Great Careers for People
Who Like
Working with People

by
Helen Mason

An Imprint of Gale Research Inc.

Copyright © 1994

Trifolium Books Inc. and Weigl Educational Publishers Limited

First published in Canada by Trifolium Books Inc. and
Weigl Educational Publishers Limited

U.S. edition published exclusively by

U·X·L

An Imprint of
Gale Research Inc.
835 Penobscot Bldg.
Detroit, MI 48226

Library of Congress Catalog Card Number 94-60780
ISBN 0-8103-9966-0

The activities in this book have been tested and are safe when carried out as suggested. The publishers can accept no responsibility for any damage caused or sustained by use or misuse of ideas or materials mentioned in the activities.

Acknowledgments

The author and the publishers wish to thank those people whose careers are featured in this book for allowing us to interview and photograph them at work. Their love for their chosen careers has made our task an enjoyable one.

Design concept: Julian Cleva
Design and layout: Warren Clark
Editors: Rosemary Tanner, Jane McNulty
Project coordinator, proofreader: Diane Klim
Production coordinator: Amanda Woodrow
Content review: Mary Kay Winter, Trudy Rising

Printed and bound in Canada
10 9 8 7 6 5 4 3 2 1

This book's text stock contains
more than 50% recycled paper.

Contents

Featured profiles

Real Estate Sales Representative

PERSONAL PROFILE

Career: Real estate sales representative. "I help people make the largest financial investment in their lives: finding and buying a home."

Interests: Interior decorating, flower arranging, and spending time with her family. "I have a dog named Chico who goes everywhere with me. He's like a child to me now that my own children are grown up."

Latest accomplishment: "I recently expanded my office in order to provide more space for my two assistants."

Why I do what I do: "I'm a naturally warm person — I like dealing with all kinds of personalities."

I am: Enthusiastic and interested in people. "I'm an achiever. Whatever I do, I want to do right. I like challenges, and I like working with others one-on-one.

What I wanted to be when I was in school: "A judge, then a cosmetician. But later on, when I was moving from one house to another, the person who was selling my property suggested that I try real estate. I did, and he was right. This is a wonderful career."

What a real estate sales representative does

"I help people buy or sell their homes," says Toni Reyes, a real estate sales representative. "Clients who want to sell their homes ask me to 'list' them. A 'listing' is an agreement to sell a piece of property. It describes the property, what it includes, and how much it costs.

"When I list a house, I need to get a lot of information from the seller," she explains. "I also measure the house and each room in it, and then measure the lot size. Using that information, I evaluate the home, and figure out a 'listing price.' Once I've signed the listing with the clients, I put a 'for sale' sign on the property," Toni continues. "Then the local real estate board takes a picture of the front of the house. This picture, and the information that I've gathered, appears in a 'listing book.' This book shows what properties are for sale in the area."

I now have to sell my listings," Toni explains. "I arrange two types of 'open houses,' one for other sales reps, and one for people who want to buy a home. I also advertise the homes in local newspapers. Some houses are even shown on TV."

Buying a home

"I also specialize in finding homes for clients who want to buy," Toni points out. "To serve my clients well, I have to know them well. I start by asking a lot of questions — about their careers, interests, and family. I can't help clients if I don't feel comfortable with them.

"Lastly, I assess their financial situation," Toni adds. I ask them about their annual income, and the amount of money they have for a down payment. Then I calculate how much money they're able to borrow from a bank or a mortgage company in order to buy a house. That way, we know what price of home to look for."

After getting to know her clients, Toni searches in the listing book for homes that match their needs and budget. "I take the clients to see several homes," she says. "At each one, they tell me what they like and don't like about it. That way, I can narrow down the choices."

Once her clients have found a home they want to buy, Toni presents their offer to the vendor. Then she talks with both the buyer and the vendor, trying to find a selling price that both will accept. When the home is sold, a percentage of the selling price is divided among the sales representatives who were involved in the deal. This percentage is called the sales rep's "commission."

Real estate jargon

Vendor: the person selling a house
Listing: the property for sale
Listing price: the price a vendor is asking for a house
Open house: a house that is for sale and open for people to visit at a certain time
Buyer: the person who buys a house
Offer: the amount of money a potential buyer offers for a house
Selling price: price at which a property sells
Mortgage: a loan that a buyer arranges in order to purchase a house
Real estate board: an association of real estate sales representatives in a certain area
Investment property: a commercial building or apartment building purchased to yield income

Toni needs a survey, some photographs, and the listing information before she can sell a house. The survey shows the precise location and size of the piece of land, as well as the location and size of any buildings.

All in a day's work

Toni describes herself as a workaholic who works seven days a week. "I usually arrive at the office between nine and nine-thirty each morning," she says. "I start with paperwork. For example, last night I listed a house. This morning, I wrote the information about the house on the listing form and passed it on to the real estate board. Then I took pictures of the interior of the house. I began to jot down ideas for the 'presentation booklet' that I give to people who might be interested in buying the property. Next, I wrote a thank-you card and arranged a small gift for clients who had just moved into their new home."

Organizing time with clients

"While I'm doing paperwork at my desk, the phone rings constantly," Toni says. "Some calls are from new clients who've seen my newspaper or television ads and are interested in one of the homes. Other calls are from previous clients who want to sell or buy a house. I make arrangements to meet with new clients. I also arrange to show some of the houses I've listed.

"Most of my client appointments are in the evening and on weekends," Toni adds. "Often, this is the only time that working people can see the property."

Research what's available

"Every day, I go to several open houses," Toni says. "These are at homes that other sales reps have up for sale. I make notes about each one, and look for homes that might appeal to my clients.

"Advertising a home for sale is important," says Toni. "My presentation booklets show and describe the rooms in ways that will attract buyers. Luckily, my husband is a good photographer, so he takes most of the photos. I choose the angles of the photos, and may sometimes move furniture and accessories to provide atmosphere. I want buyers to think of the home in a positive way."

KITCHEN

Feast your eyes next on this State-Of-The-Art kitchen displaying its traditional white cupboards, white triple sink with garburator, jennair gas burners and built-in barbecue, jennair gourmet oven and much, much more.
Truly an entertainer's delight.

THE LIVING ROOM

Enter the unique formal sitting room, adjacent to the entrance. This room is separate, having its own personality and is truly a special place.
The richly stained dark parquet floor is complimented with colonial baseboards and cornice moulding. The four separated windows are complimented by white macro venetian looking out to this quiet court.

THE FOYER

As you enter through the front door with the light streaming through the windows you are eloquentley met with a large, formal, breath-taking entrance way.
Observe the large 14" X 14" marble-look ceramic tiles, the rich looking dark stained staircase that spans three floors and instantly feast your eyes on the large stately dining area.

It's a Fact

Most North Americans spend about 32 percent of their gross income on housing. For those who own their homes, housing costs include mortgage payments, property taxes, and maintenance and repairs.

"Every two weeks, I do an in-office 'duty day.' This involves answering calls from people who are interested in buying and selling. Last month, I got a call from a woman who lived 2000 miles away. She was moving to my city, and wanted a home in a quiet neighborhood, on a lot with mature trees, close to public transportation. She arranged to fly in and meet me. Before she arrived, I visited many homes looking for one she might like. My research narrowed the field to six homes, and I sent her pictures of each one. When she arrived, I showed her the properties, and she bought a home in three days!"

According to Toni, her days are often quite long and unpredictable. "Usually, I meet my husband for lunch. Then I work until around 9:30 in the evening. Often I'm not home until after ten, or even midnight. Not

all real estate sales reps work the long hours I do," Toni adds. "You can make a good living working fewer hours per week. I work longer because I like to do everything extremely well!"

Some real estate sales reps specialize in managing properties owned by their clients. They arrange the rental of houses, condominiums, or even vacation cottages like this one.

Activity

Home for sale

Toni spends a lot of time advising clients about how to prepare their home for sale. She measures each room, photographs different views of the home and the rooms, and writes appealing descriptions. What does she have to keep in mind while doing this? Find out for yourself by trying the following activity. You will prepare promotional material for selling a home.

You will need
camera and film
measuring tape
paper and art materials
glue or tape

Procedure
1. First, choose the home that you will work with. This could be a large historical home open to the public, a tiny apartment, or even your own home. Obtain permission to tour it, measure the rooms, and take photographs. Tour the home, looking for the most attractive views of each room. Photograph these views.
2. Measure each room.
3. Read how Toni described the rooms in the presentation booklet shown on page 6. Write a description for each of your photographs. As you write, consider the following:
   - What words will encourage people to imagine their own family living in the home?
   - Use positive words that emphasize the value of the home and how it is decorated. For example, a small room might be referred to as "cosy," and a large room as "spacious."
   - Consider the age and the lifestyle of the people who might be interested in the home you're advertising. Mention features of the home that will appeal to this group.
4. Use your pictures, descriptions, and measurements to develop a brochure or a presentation booklet to make an advertisement for the home.
5. Ask several people to evaluate your sales promotion. What suggestions do they have that might make your advertising more effective?

How to become a real estate sales representative

There are many ways to start in any sales job. Selling real estate is no exception. Toni suggests taking business-related courses, including English, marketing, and consumer studies in high school. "A knowledge of mathematics is also important," she says. "For example, you have to understand what interest is, and how to calculate interest, so that you can explain mortgages and interest rates to your clients."

Professional training

Real estate sales representatives must be licensed. To earn their licenses, applicants take several courses that teach them the basics of real estate. "The courses I took were useful but difficult," Toni recalls. "They included selling, mortgages, and how to develop advertising methods and client services. They also explained the laws related to buying and selling property. We were also taught how to 'appraise' or evaluate properties. There were a lot of details, and I know many people who had to take the courses several times before passing them. Once they did, though, they became successful real estate sales reps."

Some areas have a "probation" or "articling" period for real estate sales reps. During this period, licensees are expected to take additional courses. "Since requirements for qualification can vary from area to area, it's best to check with your local real estate board," Toni suggests. "Ask someone at a nearby real estate office for the telephone number of the real estate board."

Interested in interest?

Interest is the amount of money that people pay when they borrow money from a bank, a trust company, or a private investor. At 7 percent interest, borrowers pay $7 per year for every $100 they borrow. At a rate of 7 percent, how much interest would be charged on a mortgage of $50 000? To find out, multiply $50 000 times 0.07. Check your answer with the one on page 48.

Is this career for you?

"Buying a home is the largest investment most people make in their whole lives," Toni says. "Buyers have to trust their sales rep. It's important that a rep be honest, sincere, and warm. These traits encourage people to have confidence in you.

"I listen to clients and watch their body language," she adds. "If people seem to be holding back, I tell them, 'Don't worry about finding a home. It's my job to find the best possible home for you for the best possible price.' And I do just that."

Real estate sales reps keep in constant touch with clients whose property they have listed. Such clients are anxious to sell their property for the highest possible price. Toni keeps them informed about similar homes that have sold, and the selling prices of these homes.

Know your area

"I drive clients around to show them homes in many parts of the city. To do this, I have to know the city well," Toni advises. "They wouldn't be too impressed if we got lost!" she laughs.

Self-confidence is vital

"It's important to be confident in yourself," Toni comments. "For beginners in real estate, that can be difficult. Here's a tip I picked up from another successful sales rep. 'Fake it 'til you make it,' she advises. That means acting confident, but *not* pretending to be something you're not. It also means complimenting yourself on what you do well. This builds your self-esteem. You can become what you tell yourself you are."

Career planning

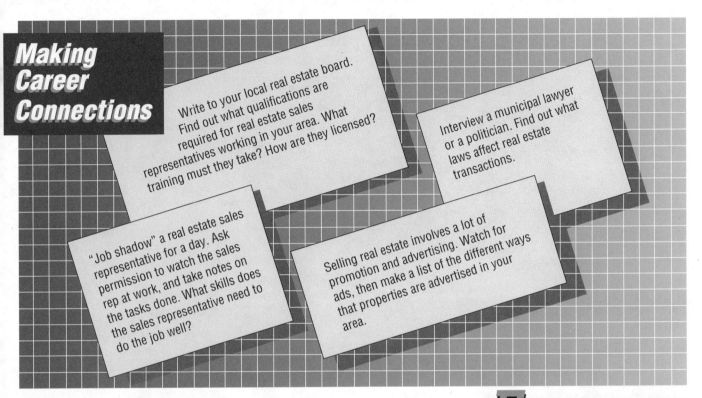

Making Career Connections

Write to your local real estate board. Find out what qualifications are required for real estate sales representatives working in your area. What training must they take? How are they licensed?

Interview a municipal lawyer or a politician. Find out what laws affect real estate transactions.

"Job shadow" a real estate sales representative for a day. Ask permission to watch the sales rep at work, and take notes on the tasks done. What skills does the sales representative need to do the job well?

Selling real estate involves a lot of promotion and advertising. Watch for ads, then make a list of the different ways that properties are advertised in your area.

Getting started

Interested in being a real estate sales representative? Here's what you can do now.

1. Volunteer to work with a real estate sales representative.
2. Learn a second language. Consider French, Spanish, German, Chinese, or Japanese.
3. Find out about real estate in other countries.
4. Join a social club. In sales, you'll need a lot of experience meeting and getting along with all types of people.
5. Learn to budget your money. Real estate sales representatives have "good" years and "bad" years, depending on how many homes they sell.
6. In high school, take mathematics, English, geography, history, and business courses. Pay particular attention to how interest rates are calculated.

Related careers

Here are some related careers you may want to check out.

Interior decorator
Applies the client's interests and ideas to develop plans for decorating a business or a home.

General contractor
Follows plans to build or renovate commercial and residential buildings. Serves as a link between the client and tradespeople, such as carpenters, electricians, and plumbers.

Title searcher
Usually works for a law firm. Does research to find out who legally owns a piece of property, and whether any money is still owing on it.

Mortgage broker
Arranges mortgage financing (loans) for real estate buyers. Some brokers work in financial institutions; others work on their own and are paid a fee for this service.

Future watch

"It's very difficult for individual vendors to negotiate a good deal with individual buyers, without the help of a real estate expert," Toni advises. "For this reason, real estate sales reps will continue to be needed to assist vendors in selling property, and buyers in buying property." In the future, real estate sales representatives may provide more services to clients, such as arranging mortgages, managing investment properties, and making recommendations for renovations or redecorating.

Kevin Lee

Social Work Supervisor

PERSONAL PROFILE

Career: Social work supervisor. "I help to manage a social services agency that provides services to residents in the area. There's an AIDS awareness program, care facilities for children and senior citizens, and an after-school program for young people."

Interests: The outdoors. "I love taking my family and friends fishing. I also enjoy wilderness canoe tripping."

Latest accomplishment: "I helped develop a game that focuses on AIDS and drug education. It's being distributed to schools and youth programs."

Why I do what I do: "I grew up in a downtown area where I had to adjust to a new culture. I like helping people who are going through the same adjustment."

I am: Sometimes an extrovert, sometimes more reserved. "I have a slight stutter but it doesn't bother me. I think I have good communication skills: I listen to what others say and try to see things from their point of view."

What I wanted to be when I was in school: A minister. "But I took a business course, and was a collection agent before I went into social work."

What a social work supervisor does

Kevin Lee works for a large social services agency in the downtown area of a city. "The agency provides recreational and social opportunities, skill training, shelter, and employment for more than 14 000 people in a diverse community," he explains. "The agency also feeds the homeless, teaches English, runs an after-school drop-in program for young people, and helps people who are victims of family violence."

As the assistant executive director of the agency, Kevin supervises the work of more than 100 staff. "I meet with staff members regularly," says Kevin. "We discuss any problems they're having and try to come up with solutions. For example, our youth employment agency was having trouble finding jobs for young people. The manager and I discussed the problem. Then we developed a computer course for English as a second language, so that teens could learn English and computer skills at the same time.

Brainstorming

"To help our staff think of new and different ideas, I often lead them in brainstorming sessions," Kevin says. "Spontaneous

thinking is the key. First, we list as many ideas as possible without criticizing any of them. Sometimes this means expanding on other people's ideas. We all suggest ideas, even ones that seem silly or unusable. Someone else might hear an idea and realize how to develop it. After we have recorded all the ideas, we examine what we have.

"As an example of successful brainstorming, let me tell you about our posters," Kevin smiles proudly. "When AIDS first became a problem in our area, we realized that we had brochures and posters that couldn't be used by some members of our community. Many of our clients speak only Chinese or Italian. No information about AIDS was available in either of these languages.

"At a staff meeting," Kevin continues, "we brainstormed what we could do about it.

A tai-chi program organized by a social services agency helps elderly Chinese feel at home in the community. In China, many people start the day with tai-chi exercises.

Finally, we designed some AIDS awareness programs for our Italian- and Chinese-speaking clients."

A game with a purpose

"In another brainstorming session, we realized that we didn't have a good method to help young people learn about AIDS," says Kevin. "So, we decided to develop a game.

"First, we needed funding, so I appealed to the community. I talked to politicians, to the press, and to concerned citizens.

"I knew I needed help from a cross-section of the community," Kevin says. "So, I hired ten teenagers from various schools, communities, and income levels."

The teens interviewed a range of people with different viewpoints on AIDS: street people, medical experts, and AIDS patients. They also analyzed different games, then visited a toy company and interviewed the chief designer.

The group proposed five different games. They tested these games with their classmates, their friends, and their families. Based on this feedback, they chose one game, which they modified and improved.

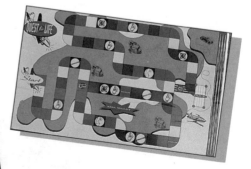

This educational game, developed by Kevin's teen group, is now being manufactured and distributed to schools and youth groups.

All in a day's work

There are no really typical days in Kevin's job. "Every day is different. That's what makes my job so challenging — and so much fun.

"We have many staff members and volunteers working in more than a dozen different locations," explains Kevin. "With so many people and so many buildings, things can go wrong. I do a lot of troubleshooting. For instance, I got to work at 8:45 this morning to discover three problems. First, there was a flood in one of the offices. Second, the police wanted a file on one of our clients. Third, the executive director was sick and couldn't go to an important meeting this evening.

"The first problem was easy to solve. One of our offices has large windows that extend to ground level. Someone had jumped against the window and cracked the join at the bottom. It rained last night, and the water flooded the floor. I asked a member of the custodial staff to caulk the windows. Later, we'll put on a grill to keep people farther away from the windows.

"Concerning the second problem: Dealing with police is discussed in our Policy and Procedures Manual. Our policy is not to hand over files, because our relationship with each client is considered confidential. Of course, if the police have a search warrant, we have to cooperate with them. I asked to see the police officers' search warrant before I gave them the file."

The third problem — the absence of the executive director — is a critical one. "A regular meeting of the finance committee is planned for this evening. Since the director can't be there, I'll attend the meeting in her place. It's too important not to go — the finance committee makes sure we have enough money to pay for all our activities.

"My work days do include a lot of meetings," explains Kevin. "At staff meetings, we discuss our plans for upcoming programs. At meetings with politicians and government officials, I explain how we spend the tax money we receive. At the same time, I can request funding for new projects."

Conflict resolution

No matter how well people get along, disagreements can arise. Kevin often helps people deal with conflicts and teaches classes in "conflict resolution."

"The conflict resolution process I use was developed in California," he

Kevin takes a few minutes out of a busy day to play a game with Frank, a worker at the drug-free arcade that offers an after-school program for young people.

notes. "This process can help two friends, family members, neighbors, or co-workers learn to get along better."

Kevin outlines the steps in the process. "First, I hear what each person, individually, has to say about the problem. I don't judge, because I want to understand how each person sees the problem, and how each one feels. Then, I ask if the person wants to repeat the explanation to the other party," he says. "If both people want to do that, if they want to find a way to resolve their differences, I arrange a meeting between them.

"I attend as a third party, and I set down rules for the meeting," Kevin explains. "Both parties must agree to listen to the other person without interrupting, and must respect the other person's point of view. Once they have agreed to this, I help them communicate how they feel about what has happened. I try to point out any similarities in what they have said. This helps them understand the other person's point of view.

"I don't suggest any solutions. Instead, I encourage the parties involved to suggest their own solutions to the conflict. If people think up their own solutions, the remedy usually lasts longer than one that has been decided by someone else, or ruled by a court of law."

Reports and paperwork

Kevin also does one or two hours of office work each day. "I plan the annual report," he says. "This report is like my agency's report card. It provides a summary of the work we've done throughout the year. The report includes information about the services we offer. This year the services include AIDS information, a drop-in program, and an agency for youth employment.

"Usually I finish work around 5:30 p.m.," Kevin adds. "I work three evenings a week, and I take work home on Saturdays. That makes a long week, but I wouldn't have it any other way."

Activity

Resolving conflicts

With two other students, role-play a conflict resolution scenario. This activity may help you develop some strategies to use whenever you encounter a conflict with a friend, family member, or co-worker.

1. Decide on a problem that might cause conflict. For example, your brother wears your clothes without permission, then throws them on the bedroom floor.
2. Discuss the two points of view you and your brother might have on this subject. For example, you might be angry because your clothes aren't clean and ready to wear when you want them. Your brother might assume he can wear your clothes because you always use his sports equipment.
3. As a group, discuss what the conflict is about. What words and actions might you use to express your point of view? What might your brother do and say?

4. Have one member of the group play "you," while another plays "your brother" and the third member plays the "third party."
5. The third party meets privately with each individual and listens to each side of the story.
6. Role-play a three-person meeting. What can the third party say and do to help the people in conflict see each other's side of the situation?
7. After a few minutes, stop the role-play and discuss what else the third party might say or do to help the others find a solution. Experiment until your group finds a strategy that feels appropriate.
8. Change roles, and have the two people role-playing the conflict create another conflict scenario. Again, the third party mediates, using some of the problem-solving techniques from Step 7.
9. Make a list of several steps that you and your friends can take when trying to resolve conflicts.

How to become a social work supervisor

Kevin originally planned to specialize in business. "I was working as the collection officer for a condominium. One day I met a tenant who couldn't work because he had broken his arm," he recalls. "His wife was ill, his child was crying, and there was no food in the house. I was supposed to give the man notice to leave the apartment. Instead, I told him where he could get help. Then I quit my job and went back to college to study social work.

"Depending on the type of job they want, social workers may need different kinds of education," Kevin explains. "Some of my co-workers are high school drop-outs. But, if you want a highly responsible job or a job in administration, you'll need a degree in social work."

A variety of experience helps

His experience in business helps Kevin in his current job. "I know how to organize my work and write reports. Business also helped me develop skills in supervising other people."

Kevin believes that his experience in other fields of social work was helpful, as well. "I started by working with developmentally challenged adults," he recalls. "I helped my clients learn life skills such as cooking, banking, and doing laundry. Later, I developed programs for young people.

"In high school physical education class, we learned how to teach a skill by breaking it down into steps," notes Kevin. "Now, when I have to teach skills to other people, or teach other people how to teach, I break the skills down into steps, too."

Kevin believes that courses in English, mathematics, and social sciences are also useful in pursuing a career in social work. "English courses help improve speaking and writing skills. Math courses assist in understanding budgets and finances. Social sciences introduced me to various theories about how people develop, think, and behave. This knowledge has helped me to work successfully with people of all ages."

Two of Kevin's staff members practice karate in a local park. Many social agencies offer lessons in team sports, crafts, swimming, and the martial arts.

I s this career for you?

According to Kevin, social work attracts all kinds of personalities. "The only similarity is that everyone in this profession likes people. They want to be involved with people, to understand more about them, and to help them.

"Different kinds of people tend to choose different areas of social work," Kevin comments. "People who enjoy working with individuals or small groups of people tend to choose jobs in 'clinical' social work. They work in hospitals or social agencies, counseling families and individuals.

"People who thrive on variety and who enjoy working with larger groups of people might work in community development," he adds. "Other social workers are employed by institutions such as school boards, government agencies, and jails."

People skills are vital

According to Kevin, "people skills" are of more importance to social workers than educational level. "You have to know how to get along with people from many different backgrounds. In my job, I deal with everyone from homeless people on the street to the mayor of the city. It's important to consider people from all walks of life as valuable members of the community."

Career planning

Making Career Connections

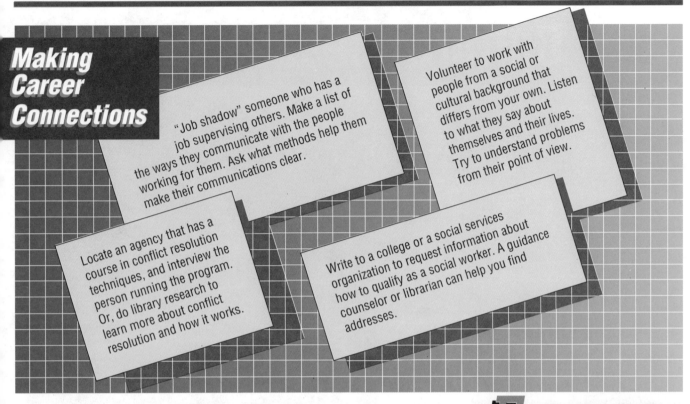

"Job shadow" someone who has a job supervising others. Make a list of the ways they communicate with the people working for them. Ask what methods help them make their communications clear.

Volunteer to work with people from a social or cultural background that differs from your own. Listen to what they say about themselves and their lives. Try to understand problems from their point of view.

Locate an agency that has a course in conflict resolution techniques, and interview the person running the program. Or, do library research to learn more about conflict resolution and how it works.

Write to a college or a social services organization to request information about how to qualify as a social worker. A guidance counselor or librarian can help you find addresses.

Getting started

Interested in being a social work supervisor? Here's what you can do now.

1. Many social agencies require volunteers. Learn about the types of volunteer jobs involved, and work in an area that appeals to you.
2. Join clubs with regular formal meetings. Participation will help you learn ways to make formal recommendations, draw up an agenda, and chair a meeting.
3. Read local newspapers to learn about events and programs in your community.
4. Join a political organization. Find out how agencies, groups, and individuals persuade politicians to make decisions and pass laws.
5. In high school, take English, mathematics, and physical education.

Related careers

Here are some related careers you may want to check out.

Child care worker
Works in a day care facility or a nursery school. Takes care of children while their parents are at work.

Politician
Elected by voters to serve in a particular level of government. Tries to develop programs and make laws to satisfy the wants and needs of voters.

Guidance counselor
Works at schools and employment centers. Helps students and clients to identify the job-related skills they possess, and the types of work that might interest them. Locates courses and other training that lead toward these areas of employment.

Recreation director
Works in hospitals, senior citizens' homes, day care facilities, prisons, or other people-oriented agencies.

Future watch

As people strive for an improved quality of life, social work will continue to grow in importance. People who are having personal problems will contact social workers to help them find ways to lead happier and more productive lives. As the average age of our population increases, more people will live in senior citizens' homes and nursing homes, where many of their needs will be identified and met by social workers.

Fran Tabobondung

Cultural Researcher

PERSONAL PROFILE

Career: Cultural researcher. "I'm working on a community-based project involving five First Nations and a board of education. My job is to collect information and history that help teachers and both native and non-native students to understand the aboriginal perspective. This material is used in the board's elementary schools."

Interests: Baseball and aerobics. "And I enjoy listening to elders talk about what life was like during their youth."

Latest accomplishment: "I've just finished my second degree, this one in social work. The program has sharpened my insights into how people think and feel."

Why I do what I do: "I like helping teachers to understand our culture and the native point of view so that they can help their students to understand us better."

I am: "Shy and quiet, until I get to know someone. When I feel comfortable with people, I'm friendly and outgoing."

What I wanted to be when I was in school: An administrator. "But then I took a course in public administration and discovered it dealt mainly with mathematics and statistics. I was more interested in people, so I changed to anthropology and native studies."

What a cultural researcher does

In order for people to understand other cultures, they sometimes need to look at things from different points of view. Fran Tabobondung is a cultural researcher. In her work, she identifies points of view held by members of her aboriginal society. She then shares what she has learned with teachers, and encourages them to include native perspectives in classroom activities.

Fran's job has three major parts. "First, I collect oral information from elders and analyze what this tells about our local culture," she explains. "Second, I interview the elders and ask questions about their customs. Finally, I help teachers to understand these traditions and encourage them to share this understanding with their students."

Collecting stories

"I spend a lot of time visiting and talking to elders," says Fran. "I meet with them, arrange to interview them, and then tape-record what they say." The stories told by the elders highlight what is important in their culture. As a comparison, think of the stories your family tells. Do you have a favorite funny story, or maybe an embarrassing one about something you did when you were young? Families use stories to pass their culture, their history, their beliefs, and their values from generation to generation.

"It's part of my job to encourage members of our group to tell their stories so that I can write them down," Fran explains. "Many elders follow ancient customs about telling stories. I respect tradition and personal beliefs by waiting until they're ready to share their stories with me."

Many history books refer to the "discovery" of North America by European explorers 500 years ago. But archeological evidence shows that people have lived in North America for at least 40 000 years — or from "time immemorial" as the elders describe it. Rock paintings and carvings across the continent show evidence of a rich way of life.

Interviewing elders

Fran also interviews elders to find out about traditional ways. She points out that her upbringing taught her to listen and learn, rather than to ask questions. This makes it difficult for her to think of questions during an interview. "That's why I plan each interview carefully," she says.

"I start with a list of questions," Fran explains. "For example, I ask what type of animals were hunted, trapped, and fished."

After she has tape-recorded the interview, she listens to the tapes and writes down what the elders said. "This is important, because a lot of our traditions aren't written down," Fran remarks.

Assisting teachers

"From my tapes, I make summaries of what I think is important in different subject areas," Fran continues.

She sends a summary of the information she has gathered to the teachers who plan the curriculum, or set courses for the schools in her area. The teachers work with her and a group of elders to develop material for use in elementary schools.

Behavior reflects culture

In some cultures, it's polite for people to look each other in the eye when they are speaking. Members of other cultures, such as some groups of aboriginal people, keep their eyes lowered as a sign of respect when someone older or more influential is speaking to them. What happens when people from these two cultures talk to each other? The people who look others in the eye might think that those who don't are not listening. On the other hand, the people who avoid eye contact might think that people who meet their gaze are being rude or forward. When people from different cultural backgrounds discuss why they behave in the ways that they do, they have less trouble understanding one another.

All in a day's work

Fran spends a lot of her day arranging, conducting, and keeping track of interviews. "I really enjoy the interviews," she comments. "Many elders show me interesting artifacts, or items made by people in the past. Some give me gifts, because an exchange of gifts is part of our tradition. I will eventually give each elder a cup with a logo specially designed for our project."

This logo was developed by George King, an aboriginal high school student. The five feathers represent the five First Nations that joined with the local board of education to hire Fran. "The clasped hands represent young people working with elders," explains Fran. "The hands also symbolize native and non-native people working together."

Preserving the past

Many aboriginal peoples have shared their traditional ways of life with historians. In 1914, Ishi, a member of the Yahi people in California, guided two anthropologists into the bush to teach them Yahi methods of hunting and fishing. Ishi was the last member of his people. If he hadn't taught anthropologists about the Yahi way of life, his culture would have died with him.

Fran usually talks to an elder for a while before turning on the tape recorder. "If the elder doesn't want to be taped, I take notes during the interview," Fran cautions. "It's hard to listen, think, and write at the same time. But it's important to consider the people you're interviewing, and respect their feelings and beliefs. If turning off my tape recorder makes someone feel more comfortable, then that's what I do."

Analyzing stories

After each interview, Fran listens to the tapes and makes a computer "log" of what has been said. "This is the tedious part of the work," she admits.

Fran reflects on what the stories mean in aboriginal society. "Oral history includes many types of stories. Through them, our people pass on values, history, spirituality, and life experiences."

Fran points out that many people hear or read native stories, then make up their own similar tales or legends. She thinks that this shows disrespect. "Stories should be retold exactly the way they are heard. They should not be written down or taped without permission."

Deciding what to use

Once Fran has logged the stories and the interviews, she works with a group of teachers to decide how the material will match with various school subjects. Accounts of how aboriginal peoples grew corn and squash, for example, belong in science. Story telling is part of language arts.

Fran makes some suggestions about how to use information, but, she emphasizes, "it's the teachers

Howard Contin grew up in the bush, then lived in a city for 40 years before returning to the place where he was born. He is currently writing a book titled *Reflections from the Sweat Lodge Fire*, about how native ways helped him to counsel people struggling with personal problems. Here, he explains to Fran that the three strands of the sweetgrass braid represent the three aspects of humanity: mind, body, and spirit.

who will make the final decisions about what they will use in class."

As the teachers develop ideas and units for using the information Fran has collected, Fran checks the accuracy of the material with a group of elders. "The elders are the experts and the best people to comment on how well we are reflecting actual teachings and beliefs."

Fran points out that it's important for students to hear about ideas and attitudes from many cultures. Showing different points of view helps students gain self-respect

Fran listens to a tape and logs the information on her computer. She identifies each person being interviewed, the number of the tape, and the side.

because they see that their beliefs and ideas can be shared, and have value.

"If I can help teachers perceive how the local aboriginal people think and feel, they'll be better prepared to

get these ideas across to their students," she says. "For example, a story about fishing might reflect the traditional concern for the environment. If students think about these concerns, and realize that their own ideas differ, they might begin to question why they think the way they do. This is an important step in beginning to understand yourself — and others."

Activity

Trace your family history

There are several different ways to collect cultural and historical information. Many people are interested in family stories. Others are more interested in names, places, and dates. The following activity will give you an opportunity to experiment with both methods of collecting data.

You will need
tape recorder
several older family members, or
    members of your community

Listen to oral stories
1. Visit some older members of your family. If you have no older relatives, or if they live too far away, it can be just as interesting to visit other older people in your community.
2. Ask the people if you may tape-record the conversation.

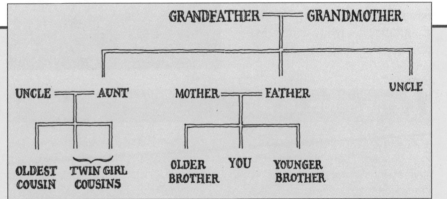

Encourage them to tell stories about when they were young: the games they played, how they spent their evenings, the friends they had, and so on.
3. When you listen to the tape later, analyze what the stories suggest is important to the speakers.

Collect names and dates
1. Interview family members on both sides of your family, or some older people living in your community.
2. Gather information about the names, birth dates, and death dates of as many family members as possible.

3. Try to design a "family tree" for at least three generations. This diagram shows one way that you might organize the information you've gathered.

Which method do you prefer?
1. Compare what you learned by listening to stories with what you learned by researching a family tree.
2. Which method of research do you find more interesting?
3. Which type of information do you think is more important?

How to become a cultural researcher

Fran has always been interested in people. As a teenager, she spent many hours listening to stories told by her tribal elders. She also visited other tribes and listened to their stories. "Playing competitive sports was a good way to make contacts among the members of other tribes," she recalls.

In high school, Fran concentrated on history, English, and mathematics. "I am interested in working with people in many different ways. So I earned one degree in anthropology and native studies, and another in social work."

Respect leads to trust

"In my job, I have to gain people's trust," Fran continues. "When I'm working with elders, I have learned to wait until they are ready to talk. My interviews often start with a cup of

coffee and a brief chat. This shows respect for the people. As they get to know and trust me, they are more willing to share their knowledge."

Fran also explains the purpose of the interview, and how she is able to safeguard the information she receives. "The logged tapes are returned to the aboriginal groups for their archives, a museum containing historical documents. That reassures the elders that we follow through in sharing their ideas with others, and protect their privacy."

Fran says that body movements, voice, and language are all important parts of story telling. Here, Howard Contin tells a story about the stones in his sweat lodge. He says that the stones represent the important moral and spiritual values held by his people. These include wisdom, love, respect, bravery, honesty, humility, and truth.

Is this career for you?

According to Fran, in a career like hers, it's important not to judge people. "There are many differences between and within every cultural group. We need to respect these differences."

"If you didn't grow up in the community you're studying, it's a good idea to learn to be a 'participant-observer,'" suggests Fran. "Learn the history of the community. This will help you understand the social, economic, spiritual, and physical roots. It is then important to take part in the life of the community. Observe it, and try to see things from the participants' point of view."

Developing a network

"Part of my work involves forming a network of contacts," Fran explains. "The fact that my grandmother was a local Chief helps here. I also attended a large gathering of elders of our region where I talked to many people. By listening and asking questions, I found out many things about their communities. In addition, I discovered that a group in Minnesota is working on a similar project to ours. We're

now sharing ideas and information. I also keep in touch with many organizations and resource people working on projects similar to ours."

Be a participant-observer

You can practice observing a culture by studying events in your own neighborhood, home, and school. Choose a social situation that interests you, such as a family dinner, a game, a shopping trip, a class, or a wedding. Write down information about the physical setting, as well as any objects (such as tools and pieces of furniture) that are used. Observe and take notes on the actions and interactions of the people involved. What do they say? What does their conversation suggest about their values and attitudes? You might compare a formal occasion, such as a wedding, with an informal event, such as a picnic.

Career planning

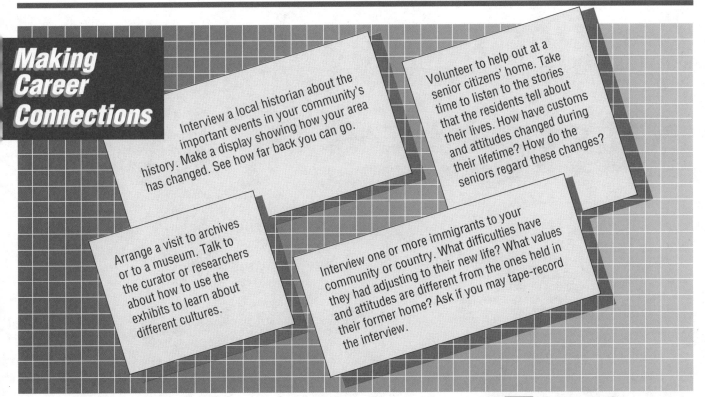

Making Career Connections

Interview a local historian about the important events in your community's history. Make a display showing how your area has changed. See how far back you can go.

Volunteer to help out at a senior citizens' home. Take time to listen to the stories that the residents tell about their lives. How have customs and attitudes changed during their lifetime? How do the seniors regard these changes?

Arrange a visit to archives or to a museum. Talk to the curator or researchers about how to use the exhibits to learn about different cultures.

Interview one or more immigrants to your community or country. What difficulties have they had adjusting to their new life? What values and attitudes are different from the ones held in their former home? Ask if you may tape-record the interview.

Getting started

Interested in being a cultural researcher? Here's what you can do now.

1. Read a variety of newspapers and magazines. Try to understand issues from many points of view.
2. Get to know people from different cultures. Listen to their ideas.
3. Become familiar with stories, folk tales, and legends from many lands. If you like, put together a collection of stories from many lands that show cross-cultural differences or similarities.
4. Some communities have storytellers' schools that offer courses in the art of storytelling. You could also start your own group for storytellers.
5. Learn the language of the people you hope to study.
6. In high school, take computer courses, social studies, and English.

Related careers

Here are some related careers you may want to check out.

Anthropologist
Studies human beings as a whole and as members of different cultures. Many anthropologists study the impact of development on traditional cultures.

Storyteller
Collects and tells stories to both children and adults. Performs at cultural events, at children's festivals, at literary events, on radio, and on television.

Human rights or employment equity coordinator
Researches the difficulties faced by people who experience discrimination in the workplace. Provides occupational counselling to members of these groups to help them progress in their jobs. Offers workshops to employers to make them more aware of how they can attract employees from under-represented groups.

Future watch

Fast electronic communication means that people throughout the world are communicating as never before. Thus, there is a growing need to help people understand one anothers' cultures. People who can help others to understand different points of view may advise business people and members of the government about how to pursue business opportunities in foreign countries. People who understand each other tend to get along better — and can also do business together.

Roy Clifton

Restaurant Manager

PERSONAL PROFILE

Career: Restaurant manager. "I greet customers as they arrive and I supervise the dining room staff. I like to treat customers as if they were guests in my own home."

Interests: Tennis, golf, mountain biking, and boating. "When I need some time to myself, I like to take a boat cruise around some nearby islands."

Latest accomplishment: "This year has been the best yet, with 80 to 90 percent repeat business at the restaurant. I feel good about that because it means our hospitality and good food are paying off."

Why I do what I do: "I love being with people. This job allows me to socialize in a pleasant and welcoming way."

I am: Flexible and easygoing, but strict in terms of job performance. "I'm strict with myself about 'work before play.' I'm also strict with staff members about how I expect them to do their jobs."

What I wanted to be when I was in school: A police officer. "I even completed a course in law and security. I was looking for a position on a police force when my brothers, who were just opening a restaurant, offered me a summer job. After two months in the business, I didn't want to leave — so here I am, seven years later."

What a restaurant manager does

Restaurant managers are responsible for the smooth running of the dining room of a restaurant. "I take care of everything that happens between the main door and the door of the kitchen," says Roy Clifton. Roy is the manager of a gourmet restaurant located beside a dock in a small vacation town.

Hiring staff

"I'm responsible for hiring staff," Roy states. "When I screen the applicants, I look for people who have had experience in the restaurant business. Personality is important, too. I want people who are outgoing. I also like employees who move quickly and who seem alert to their surroundings. People like that are often fast and efficient when they wait on tables. Of course, it's hard to tell until I observe the new employees on the job."

Training new employees

"Once I hire people, I'm responsible for training them," says Roy. "First, I want both experienced employees and new staff members to understand the philosophy of my restaurant. I explain that we strive to treat our customers like valued guests.

"Next, I hand out to them a menu information list. This list tells how various dishes are prepared, what's in each dish, and where the ingredients come from. Sometimes customers who have food allergies ask specific questions about ingredients. If the servers aren't sure about the answers, I caution them to check with me or with the kitchen staff. We need to be very careful that we don't serve anything that could cause an allergic reaction.

"It's also important for our new employees to understand the routines of the dining room. For example, a different homemade soup is prepared every day. Servers find out which 'soup of the day' is being served, and they mention it to customers when they hand out the menus.

"Because many people appreciate regular routines, I train all the staff in the restaurant to treat all of the customers in the same way."

Staff schedules

"Once the employees have been trained, I schedule their shifts around the hours that we're open," says Roy. "This can be tricky, because I

Rod Young works behind the scenes preparing a dessert tray. Rod's parents own a small fast-food takeout place. His experience in the family business helped him to get a job at the restaurant that Roy manages.

have to figure out when our busy hours are likely to occur, and line up extra staff for those times. But I also don't want employees standing idle during the slow periods when the restaurant is almost empty.

"Because I supervise 17 dining room employees — ten people per shift — and deal with hundreds of customers each week, I have to get along with many different kinds of people," Roy points out. "I often watch body language, which helps me gauge a person's mood. If I notice that a staff member is upset, I take time to talk to that person. I also speak tactfully with customers who have complaints, so I can prevent problems from recurring.

"Customer relations are usually fairly simple, such as informing people how long they'll have to wait for a table," Roy adds. "I usually try to strike up a conversation while customers are waiting. Since we're located in a vacation area, I ask them about their holiday. Or, I suggest that they fill in the time by strolling on the dock or browsing through the gift shop next door."

Marla hands out a menu shortly after she welcomes a customer.

All in a day's work

"I arrive each morning at 10 o'clock, an hour before the restaurant opens for the day," says Roy. "Right away, I make sure the staff has arrived, the tables are set, and the outdoor patio is clean.

"At 11 o'clock, I post myself at the entrance. If a lot of customers start arriving at once, a host or hostess assists me. Usually, the host or hostess is a little too young to be a server, but is in training for that position. They show people to their tables, hand out menus, and help to push tables together for larger groups."

From 11 a.m. to 3 p.m., Roy greets and takes care of the lunchtime crowd. "I seat customers either inside or on the patio, whichever they prefer. When it gets really busy, I move constantly around the restaurant, observing the customers and checking that everything is going smoothly. It's important to notice who wants dessert and who is ready for the bill."

Between 3 p.m. and 5 p.m., business slows down. "That's when I eat," smiles Roy. "That's also when I do the business banking and run any personal errands. Meanwhile, the staff clean up and prepare for the dinner shift."

"Between 5 p.m. and 10 p.m., I'm back at the entrance to greet the supper crowd," continues Roy. "I eat my own meal after 10 o'clock, when things slow down. Usually, I sit down with my brothers and discuss our upcoming plans. At 11 o'clock, I close up. I check the paperwork while the staff finish serving the last customers, clear the tables, and clean up."

Just before closing...

"Most days, I work until about midnight or 1 a.m. It takes a lot of time to schedule the staff and check the accounts," Roy comments. "I'm

How to serve in the restaurant Roy manages

1. Greet the customers.
2. Ask them if they'd like to order a beverage.
3. Mention the soup of the day as you hand out the menus.
4. Serve the beverages while the customers study the menu.
5. Ask politely if the customers are ready to order, or whether they need a few more minutes.
6. Take the food order. Ask the customers if they'd like to start with an appetizer.
7. Place the food order in the kitchen.
8. Check the table regularly to refresh beverages, pour water, and find out what else the customers might need.
9. Clear the table when the customers have finished eating the main course.
10. Bring out the dessert tray.
11. Serve dessert and tea or coffee.
12. Present the bill and thank the customer.

Roy observes what people are wearing when they arrive at the restaurant. People dressed in casual clothes are usually on holiday and in no hurry. Those in more formal clothes may be headed for a play or a concert, and they may need to finish their meal quickly.

also responsible for ordering everything that's used in the dining room. I write up a regular liquor order so that the customers can have the brands and mixed drinks they request. Also, I like to keep a good stock of fruit juices, bottled waters, pops, and non-alcoholic coolers."

Between April 1 and September 30, Roy works seven days a week. Since his business is located in a summer tourist area, he takes his holidays during the winter. "Between October and March, I work five or six days a week, then take a month off."

During slack periods, servers make sure that the condiment containers and the salt and pepper shakers are filled, ready for the next shift.

Activity

Learn to run a restaurant

To get an idea of what it might be like to manage a restaurant, try the following activity.

You will need
several cookbooks
paper
colored pencils
food ingredients for the recipes you
 choose

Procedure

1. Invite several friends or family members to a special meal a week or so from now.
2. Skim through some cookbooks and find dishes that tempt you. Select one or more from each of the following: appetizers or side dishes; entrées or main dishes; desserts; and beverages.
3. List and buy the ingredients required for each dish.
4. Keep track of how much all the ingredients cost. Also, record the total amount of time you spend planning, shopping for, preparing, and serving the meal. If you were to receive the minimum wage for your work hours, how much would you earn? Use these figures to calculate the direct costs involved in serving the meal you are preparing. What is the cost per "customer?"
5. Develop a sample restaurant menu using mouth-watering names for your dishes.
6. Draw up a timetable for cooking the meal and setting the table. The meal should be ready, but not overcooked, when your guests sit down to eat.
7. Following your timetable, prepare and cook your dishes. While the food is cooking, set out the plates and cutlery on the table.
8. When your guests arrive, greet them, and guide them to the table.
9. Offer them a beverage, then hand out the menus.
10. Serve your guests using the suggestions in the box on page 24. Try to read your guests' body language to see when they are ready for the next course in the meal.

How to become a restaurant manager

"There are many ways to become a restaurant manager," Roy remarks. "Some people get a job in a restaurant during high school. At first, they clear tables, then work their way up from servers, to shift managers, to restaurant managers."

Another route is to take business and hospitality courses in college and start out in management. Sometimes, people open their own restaurant and become manager. All these paths to restaurant management require excellent skills in getting along with people.

"In high school, take English, business courses, social sciences, and computer courses," suggests Roy. "You need to learn how to sell by suggestion to be successful in the restaurant business."

Every year, Roy upgrades his skills by taking seminars and workshops offered by business schools and hospitality organizations. "I also pick up an idea or two almost every time I visit another restaurant," he comments. "I adapt the ideas I find most useful."

Working in a restaurant in the summer as a dishwasher, or in some other job, will give you a good chance to see what the restaurant business is like.

Is this career for you?

"Not everyone can work on their feet for long hours," Roy cautions. "But long, hard hours are the norm in the restaurant business. Also, you have to be in good shape. Trays of dishes and food can be extremely heavy."

Roy doesn't mind these disadvantages, though, because he describes himself as a "people person." "I'm an extrovert who likes to be around other people all the time. That's why I love the restaurant business.

"My customers include millionaires who sail their yachts into the harbor, and campers who paddle in by canoe," he remarks. "To me, they're all the same — valued guests. I enjoy meeting people from many different backgrounds."

Expect the unexpected

Roy says it's important to be fast and flexible if you work in the restaurant business. "Sometimes I have to call an employee to ask that a schedule be changed at the last minute because we've become unexpectedly busy. At other times, business slows down and I have to send someone home early. This can be inconvenient, but flexible people can learn to enjoy the unexpected.

"The best thing about being a manager is working for myself," admits Roy. "I make my own decisions about how to deal with employees and customers. This gives me a great feeling of independence. I also feel more self-confident because the decisions I've made have resulted in a business that is growing."

Roy's colleague Lara works in the restaurant to finance her studies in food and beverage management. "This job pays my tuition and gives me experience," she explains.

Career planning

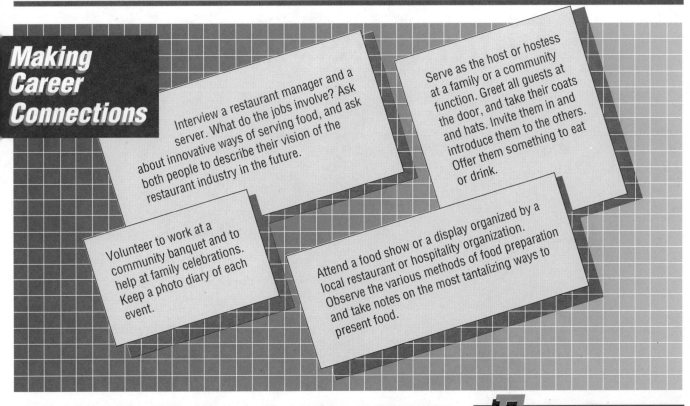

Making Career Connections

Interview a restaurant manager and a server. What do the jobs involve? Ask about innovative ways of serving food, and ask both people to describe their vision of the restaurant industry in the future.

Serve as the host or hostess at a family or a community function. Greet all guests at the door, and take their coats and hats. Invite them in and introduce them to the others. Offer them something to eat or drink.

Volunteer to work at a community banquet and to help at family celebrations. Keep a photo diary of each event.

Attend a food show or a display organized by a local restaurant or hospitality organization. Observe the various methods of food preparation and take notes on the most tantalizing ways to present food.

Getting started

Interested in being a restaurant manager? Here's what you can do now.
1. Take time to observe the restaurants where you eat. How are customers treated? What are some common routines? Do the menus make the meals sound appetizing?
2. Get a job as a dishwasher or a table hop. Many young people start out in these lower-paying restaurant jobs.
3. In high school, take cooking classes. Math, accounting, marketing, and other business courses are also relevant. English will help you with communication skills; a knowledge of computers will assist you in ordering restaurant supplies; and science can help you understand the chemical reactions that produce the delicious results on menus.

Related careers

Here are some related careers you may want to check out.

Caterer
Supplies the food for a variety of functions, such as birthday parties, weddings, and public receptions. Caterers decorate the dining area and the tables, serve guests, and clean up afterwards.

Hotel manager
Supervises the operation of a hotel. Handles everything from hiring staff, to investigating customer complaints, to ordering supplies and furnishings.

Tour escort
Conducts groups of travellers on organized tours of various locations. Assists travellers who experience problems, such as illness or lost passports. Must demonstrate patience and be excellent with people. May also work as the social director on a cruise ship.

Future watch

Surveys show that people are eating more and more meals outside the home. As a result, jobs in the restaurant business are becoming more common. These range from jobs in the fast-food industry to those in gourmet restaurants, where the customers expect fine food and elegant service. In addition, food processing companies are developing more sophisticated food items that can be heated in a microwave oven. As a result, restaurant customers are served meals more promptly and they're more likely to eat in a restaurant when they're in a hurry.

Angelika Baur

Photo Researcher

PERSONAL PROFILE

Career: Photo researcher. "I work with a team of people who develop books. My job is to find interesting photos that illustrate what the author wants to say. Great pictures help people become interested in buying the book."

Interests: Cooking, art, athletics, movies, and music. "I did my first bungee jump recently. I loved it!"

Latest accomplishment: "Last fall, the company I work for published a wonderful book for students in junior high school. The book is selling so well that we're going to print more copies of it."

Why I do what I do: "I enjoy the challenge of working with other people to make a book so exciting that customers want to buy it. When I work on textbooks, I think about what I liked when I was in school, and I look for pictures that will appeal to students."

I am: Sociable, punctual, stubborn, well-organized. "I keep notes to remind me of things I need to do."

What I wanted to be when I was in school: "A flight attendant, because I wanted to travel. I was accepted for training, but I decided I wasn't ready to move away from home."

What a photo researcher does

Have you ever thought about how books are produced? Many people assume that the authors are responsible for book production. In reality, most books are developed by a team of people working together. Angelika Baur, a photo researcher, is one member of that team.

Angelika works for a large publishing company that produces textbooks. "I'm in charge of finding the photographs to illustrate the books," says Angelika. "In my job, I talk with many different people every day."

Figuring out what's needed

"After the manuscript arrives from the author, the editor sets up a meeting with the author and me," Angelika says. "Both the author and the editor propose ideas about the pictures that are needed. I tell them about the shots I already have on file. Then, we discuss how I might research any other photos required."

The editor makes a list of the pictures needed for a book. "I study this list, then I ask the editor for advice about what each photograph should depict," Angelika says. "I want to make sure I get the correct pose, background, and atmosphere. If a specific shot is hard to find, or if it costs too much money, I may suggest an alternative."

Angelika reviews some photos with an editor. Together, they choose the ones they consider appropriate for a specific book. The book's designer will make the final selection of photos.

Locating photo sources

Where does Angelika find the photos she needs? "I start by talking to all kinds of people," she replies. "I phone companies and associations to ask if they have particular photos on file. I phone photographers who shoot certain types of photos. I also ask co-workers if they might have suitable shots in their personal collections. That's how I locate some of the great family shots we use.

"Often, my research involves telephoning people in other countries," she points out. "Fortunately, I speak German and I understand some French. There are some excellent photo suppliers in Germany and in France. Using the appropriate language to request photos can speed up an order."

Looking for "freebies"

"Photos can be expensive," Angelika comments. "Shots that are hard to find may cost up to $200 each! I recently paid a large sum of money for a picture of Galapagos turtles. The picture was expensive, but the turtles looked similar to dinosaurs — which is exactly what the author wanted. But I can only spend an average of $25 to $35 per picture. Because some shots are pricey, I look for 'freebies' to

balance the budget. This involves a lot of phoning around.

"Fortunately, I know the public relations people in many businesses," adds Angelika. "I often call these people, and explain what I need and how I want to use it. I also send a copy of the text that accompanies the photo. Companies prefer to be shown in a positive light, so they won't approve the use of a shot unless the public relations department okays the text. Sometimes I have to talk to two or three different people before I get permission to use the photo."

Book jargon

Author: an individual who writes and revises the manuscript that will be developed into a book.

Cropping: trimming a photograph to eliminate unimportant features, and to highlight only the most important item or person shown.

Designer: the "visual expert" who decides on the overall "look" of the book, including the size of the printed words and where to place the pictures.

Editor: the "word expert" who makes suggestions to the author about how to improve the writing and how to enliven the text with some photos and illustrations. Editors also correct any factual, stylistic, grammatical, and spelling errors in a manuscript.

Manuscript: the author's unedited writing that is submitted to the publisher. Most books go through several manuscript "drafts" before being published.

Photo shoot: a session during which photographs are taken in a particular location or in a studio. May involve hired models or volunteers who pose for the situation to be photographed.

All in a day's work

Angelika begins work at 8:30 a.m. "Since I'm usually working on four or five books at a time, I start with the project that needs the most attention," she explains. "On my computer, I review the list of the shots I need and what I've done to find each shot. The list shows me whom I called, when I called the person, and what we discussed. After each call, I update the list to show what we decided to do.

"My co-workers and I spend time discussing the pictures we're looking for," Angelika points out. "We often help each other to locate a special photo or the name of a new contact person. Because we all work together in an open area, we sometimes overhear each other's conversations and can make suggestions."

Editorial meetings

"Every week or so, I meet with the editors who are working on each of my projects," Angelika continues. "I bring along the list of photos and the stack that I've collected.

We examine each photo, decide which ones we like best, and discuss how they will fit into the final book. If we don't like a shot, we discuss alternatives. Sometimes the pose is wrong or the picture is out of focus. I then either look for a better picture or arrange a photo shoot to get exactly what we need."

Planning photo shoots

"To shoot photos for a book, I first make a detailed list of the photos we need, the models and locations we'd like to use, and the props we need to collect," Angelika continues. "Then I organize the shoot. I meet with the photographers to discuss how I want the photos done, and I negotiate a price with them. If I need models for some photos, I sometimes ask people at work to pose for us. It's too expensive to use professional models for most of the shots we take. Instead, I explain what I

want and I get permission from them and from their supervisor before we do the shoot.

"Next, I direct the photo shoot. This includes planning the clothing and telling the models how to pose. It's fun to do this."

Angelika asks each model to sign a "model release form," which gives her company permission to print the person's photograph in a book.

Angelika and the photographer want people to look comfortable when their picture is taken. "Sometimes, I chat with the models about something that interests them," she notes. "Once people forget that they are being photographed, they relax and look great." These pictures show Kevin Lee in two different poses. As the photo shoot progressed, he began to be more relaxed and "natural."

Paperwork also involves people

"Between meetings, I write letters to ask permission to use photos, to explain what kinds of photos I need, and to thank people for their help," comments Angelika. "I also write memos that outline the permissions I have already received, and I answer questions for the project editors. Then I write payment requisitions so that my company knows how much to pay for the photos we're using.

"My paperwork must be well organized!" she stresses. "I file all the

photos in folders, one folder for each chapter. I label the photos that we intend to use and I make notes outlining whether and how the photos need to be cropped. I send unused photos back to the sources. Then I check our own photo library to make sure that any photos I've used or looked at have been kept in order."

Angelika crops photographs to get rid of distracting details. To check the best way to crop a photo, she covers part of the photo with her hand.

Activity

Identify the book team

Books are humanity in print.
— Barbara Tuchman

For every book you read, play you see, or music album you hear, a lot of people have worked together to "make it happen." This activity will help you find out who works on a book publishing team.

You will need
this book
several textbooks with photos, drawings, and excerpts from magazines or newspapers
several popular fiction and non-fiction books

*Great Careers for People Who Like Working with People!
by Helen Mason*

Procedure

1. Open this book to the "title page," the first printed page in the book. Who wrote this book? Who published it?
2. The "copyright page" is on the reverse of the title page.
   (a) Who owns the copyright? This information is accompanied by a symbol that looks like this: ©
   (b) The "copyright notice" indicates whether you may copy material from the book. What does the copyright notice in this book say?
   (c) When was the author of this book born? List the names of the book's designer, the layout artist (the person who assembled pictures and text together on the pages), the editors (the people who worked with the writer to improve the original manuscript), and the proofreader (the person who checked that every word was spelled correctly).
   (d) "Acknowledgments" are "thank yous" to various people who have assisted in the book's publication. Who is acknowledged in this book, and why?
   (e) When was the book published?
3. The "credits" are at the back of the book, following the "index." Credits list the names of all the people and agencies who provided photos or other materials for use in the book. Who took most of the photos for this book? Who else supplied illustrations?
4. Check the title page and the credits page in other books. Try to find a book that includes copies of magazine or newspaper articles. How are these articles credited?
5. With some friends, create a display showing the titles of the various people involved in producing books. What does each person do? Also, list the name and the job description of each member of *your* team, and include acknowledgments to thank the people who helped you.

How to become a photo researcher

According to Angelika, photo researchers come from a variety of backgrounds. "The most important factor is experience in working with people," she notes. "When I call someone I don't know, I take time to develop a telephone relationship. Showing an interest in other people gives me better results."

Related education

"A high school diploma is basic to this job," Angelika points out. "But then you need additional training and experience to land a job as a photo researcher. College courses in publishing, advertising, public relations, marketing, photography, and computers are all useful. So is knowledge of a second language. Any of the common international languages — including French, German, Chinese, Japanese, Hebrew, and Arabic — can help you in this type of work.

"I've also had some modeling experience," smiles Angelika. "This helped me to understand the technical aspects of photo shoots."

"I learn a lot about people through my volunteer work," says Angelika. This little girl had an accident that paralyzed her right side. After they've played for a while, Angelika helps the child to exercise her right arm.

Angelika and an editor examine some slides on a light table. "We look for excellent focus and strong colors," says Angelika. "Exciting shots will entice readers to explore a book."

Is this career for you?

"Most photo researchers are extroverts," comments Angelika. "I interact with many different people each day, and I like to give them my undivided attention, both in face-to-face meetings, and in telephone conversations."

Angelika believes that a photo researcher must be artistic and creative, as well as organized. "I've applied my artistic sense and creativity to develop a good eye for shots that will attract readers," Angelika explains. "But without my organizational skills, I couldn't begin to keep all those photos in order!"

It's stressful at times

"I also have to handle a lot of pressure and stress," admits Angelika. "Often, I'm working on five major books at the same time. Of course, all the editors want their projects completed on time. I have to make sure that I organize my work so that each job gets its fair share of my time — and meets the deadline!

"Finally, a photo researcher has to be able to work independently," concludes Angelika. "Nobody tells me what to do each morning. I come in, I decide which job has top priority, and I do it. I love the freedom and the flexibility to plan each day as I like."

Career planning

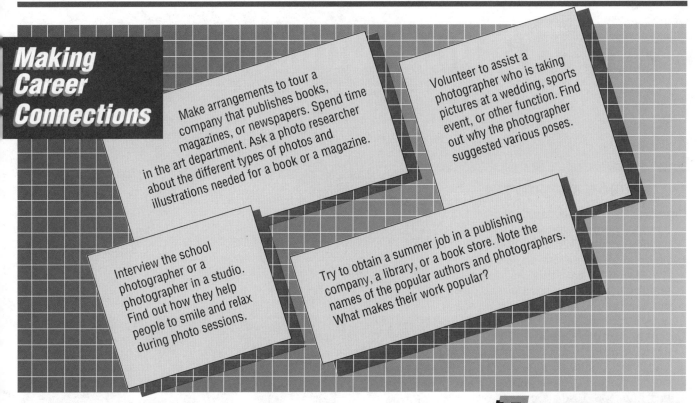

Making Career Connections

Make arrangements to tour a company that publishes books, magazines, or newspapers. Spend time in the art department. Ask a photo researcher about the different types of photos and illustrations needed for a book or a magazine.

Volunteer to assist a photographer who is taking pictures at a wedding, sports event, or other function. Find out why the photographer suggested various poses.

Interview the school photographer or a photographer in a studio. Find out how they help people to smile and relax during photo sessions.

Try to obtain a summer job in a publishing company, a library, or a book store. Note the names of the popular authors and photographers. What makes their work popular?

Getting started

Interested in being a photo researcher? Here's what you can do now.

1. When you do a research project, illustrate it with carefully chosen photos and drawings.
2. Take a business course to help you learn telephone etiquette and other office skills.
3. Learn to use computer programs for word processing and spreadsheets.
4. Read books and magazines about art, photography, and design.
5. Join a photography club. Find out how to distinguish excellent photographs from merely good ones.
6. Volunteer to work on the school yearbook to learn about book design and photo cropping.
7. In high school, study English and art. History and geography will help you learn where certain kinds of visuals might be available. Physics will help you to understand the action of light and color in photography.

Related careers

Here are some related careers you might want to check out.

Photographer
Takes photographs of various subjects and locations. Sells the photos to publishing houses, magazines, photo agencies, and other businesses. May also operate a studio.

Public relations officer
Provides information about specific businesses or products so that the public views these businesses and products in a positive way.

Customer service representative
Works for large stores, businesses, or industries. Handles customer complaints, often on the telephone.

Bookseller
Decides which materials will appeal to bookstore clients, and orders them from the publishers. Displays books in an eye-catching manner. Reads many books to be able to help customers find what they need.

Future watch

Because television encourages people to think in terms of visual images, publishers now spend more time and money looking for colorful visuals that will attract readers. Angelika says that jobs like hers are also becoming more common in video, movie, and television production.

"Some photographers now send me photographs on small computer disks. This enables me to use the computer to crop a photograph, then check my cropping by viewing a computer simulation of the book page I'm working on. I expect that my services will also be valuable to multimedia producers, such as the creators of rock music videos."

Fred Brigham

Training Consultant

PERSONAL PROFILE

Career: Training consultant. "I counsel people who want to work at jobs in the skilled trades."

Interests: Travel and physical fitness. "I do calisthenics, some weight lifting, and cardiovascular workouts. I also buy and sell real estate for profit."

Latest accomplishment: "I've accumulated enough overtime and vacation credits to go back to school for a 12-week course. I've been accepted into a course on occupational health and safety."

Why I do what I do: "These days, many people change their career several times. I've embarked on my fourth career, and I enjoy helping others make job changes, too."

I am: A doer, a risk-taker, and a persistent individual. "I don't take 'no' as a final answer. I kept applying for my current job for three years, and was interviewed several times before I was hired. To me, success is a matter of being ready for the right opportunity."

What I wanted to be when I was in school: "I had no idea. Between 15 and 22, I just bobbed along, taking any job that came my way. I worked in a pickle factory, shot pool, then worked on an assembly line. I was working at a summer camp when the director noticed my ability to interact well with people. I've grown from there."

What a training consultant does

Fred Brigham works for the training department of a large government agency. "My department deals with hundreds of skilled trades," he says. "Some of these trades, such as hairstyling and motor vehicle mechanics, are regulated by the government. People training in these fields are called 'apprentices.' Other trades, such as baking and printing, have 'voluntary certification.'

"My job is to attract people into the skilled trades," notes Fred. "I visit high schools and talk to students about the various trades available to them. I give out information about training programs, and I encourage young people to consider one of the skilled trades. I also help trainees find placements where they can learn the skills of a particular trade.

Evaluating skill levels

"Once people show interest in the trades, I help them to assess their interests and temperament," Fred explains. "I ask them basic questions, such as where and how they like to work. Then I ask about specific dislikes or fears, for example, an aversion to heights. I spend a lot of time on this assessment because it helps each client narrow down the job possibilities."

Fred also evaluates the experience of older clients who come from other countries. "I ask them about their education and experience in their trade. Then, I explain what they must do to become licensed by the government. Some may just have to pass an exam. Others may need further training, including English as a second language."

Gathering and communicating information

"I help apprentices by providing a contract that outlines their relationship with an employer," Fred says. "The contract specifies what apprentices will learn, and how much they'll be paid. I explain what the contract means, and make sure that both parties understand their responsibilities."

"In my job, using an electronic network is important," Fred comments. "I use a computer, voice mail, a fax, and a telephone answering machine. All of these help me communicate with my co-workers and with my clients. This electronic network also increases my efficiency. But I'm not completely dependent on electronic gadgets. I file paper copies of all reports as a backup. If something goes wrong with the system — which sometimes happens — it's a relief to have the information in writing."

After taking a carpentry program, Leslie now builds log houses and cottages.

Cooks or chefs are skilled tradespeople who spend a lot of time on their feet.

Assessing your occupation preferences

Answer the following questions. Then, check your answers with Fred's lists of related occupations on page 48.
1. Do you like to work with people or alone?
2. Do you like to work indoors or outdoors?
3. Do you like to work sitting down or standing up?
4. Can you handle heights?
5. Could you work underground?
6. Would you like to work with electricity?

All in a day's work

"My typical day depends on whether I'm in the office or on the road," Fred remarks. "If it's an office day, I'm up early. I commute to my health club, where I work out until about 7:30 a.m., and I reach the office about a half hour later. Sometimes I arrive earlier. I can get a lot of work done in the early morning when the phone doesn't ring.

"One day a week, I stay in the office so that anyone who is interested in the trades can come in and ask questions about opportunities and training," says Fred. "While I'm at my desk, I develop a travel plan for my next day on the road.

"On my computer, I input the contracts I've developed with employers and their apprentices. Then I confirm their schooling arrangements. It's part of my job to find trainees a placement in one of the training sessions offered in my area. I check whether the closest training school has an available opening. If there isn't one, I find the closest alternative and I arrange training for the apprentice there.

"Toward the end of each day, I write a short report outlining what I've done," he adds. "I see and talk to so many people that it's easy to get them mixed up. These reports help me to keep all the details sorted out! Daily reports also help me write a monthly report for my department."

Fred usually heads home when his office closes at 4:30 p.m. "But if someone comes in at the last minute, I serve them after hours," he says. "That's because I believe in treating people the way I like to be treated myself."

Visiting clients

"Days on the road involve a different routine," Fred points out. "I get to the office about 7:00 a.m., pick up my messages and my travel plan, and leave around 8 o'clock. I like to start early because some employers want me to talk to their employees before they get busy at the job site."

"Each visit has a specific purpose. I may meet with employers who are

Fred travels so much to visit trainees and their employers that he writes a travel plan to stay organized.

Travel plan

September 12, 199—

Time	Employer	Address	Reason for visit
8:30 a.m.	Shipman Electric	1205 Carruthers Road	sign contract with new apprentice
9:15 a.m.	Barry's Hairdressing	19 Bayfield Street	talk to owner about hiring a trainee
10:30 a.m.	Bay Plumbing	79 Gibson Street	interview new trainee transferred in from another area
11:45 a.m.	Minesing Metal	Highway 26 and Center Road	check new address of apprentice
1:30 p.m.	French's Auto Repair	1794 Little Avenue	talk to apprentice about change in school scheduling
2:15 p.m.	Hing Lee Electric	167 Cumbermere Crescent	talk to owner about expectations of employers
3:00 p.m.	City Electric	1495 Second Avenue	get proof of experience and schooling from apprentice ready to write licensing exam
4:00 p.m.	Open Roads Driving School	7508 Lawrence Avenue	meet with new apprentices to explain their contracts

thinking of hiring an apprentice, so I explain their responsibilities. I may interview apprentices who have transferred in from another area. I need to know how much experience and schooling they already have, check their contracts, and schedule the rest of their schooling. I also meet with new apprentices to explain their contracts. And I meet with any apprentices who are ready to write their licensing exams. I ask for proof of experience and schooling before making exam arrangements."

"While I'm in a shop, I answer questions apprentices may have about their training," Fred notes. "Other employees may ask me to renew their licences. That's simple. I just take their application and their fee, and process the application when I get back to the office."

From apprentice to tradesperson

An apprentice is a trainee who is working toward a license in a skilled occupation that is regulated by the government. Apprentices spend most of their work hours employed at a job site, learning from experienced tradespeople. The rest of their time is spent in a government trade school, learning theory. A tradesperson is a skilled worker who has completed apprenticeship training and has been licensed in a trade. Tradespeople bake your bread, fix your car, build your home, and print what you are reading right now.

Koreen discovered she liked hairdressing during a high school Coop program. She now works as an apprentice. The shop owner gives her a few tips as she styles a client's hair.

Activity

Interview a tradesperson

Prepare for the interview

1. Contact and ask to interview a tradesperson working in a trade you find interesting. Explain why you want to do an interview, and arrange a time and a place to meet.
2. Before the interview, make a list of questions you want to ask about the person's trade. Remember the six key words to use in any interview: who, what, where, when, how, and why. You might want to ask questions such as the following:

■ How did you become interested in this trade?

■ What education and skills are necessary?
■ Where did you train?
■ If I were to start training tomorrow, when would I finish?
■ How do people train for this trade?
■ Do you enjoy your job? Why or why not?
■ How many job openings are there in this trade?

Conduct the interview

1. Be on time. If possible, bring a portable tape recorder, and ask permission to use it.
2. Bring your question sheet with you. Begin by checking the spelling of the person's name and trade.
3. Jot down the answers given to your questions.

4. If you think of other questions to ask during the interview, ask them, and write them on your list as well.
5. When you have completed the interview, thank the tradesperson for taking the time to talk with you.

Share what you have learned

Discuss what you have learned with a friend who interviewed a different tradesperson. How are the trades similar? How do they differ? Now, with your friend, role-play the job of a training consultant. Ask your friend — the "client" — the assessment questions on page 35, and describe the trades your friend's interests might match.

How to become a training consultant

"Training consultants come from a variety of backgrounds. What they have in common is their ability to get along with people," Fred observes. "Some have college training in general arts, social sciences, or teaching. Often they have a particular interest in the trades, or have researched trade-related issues. Many consultants specialize in one trade.

"I have both theoretical and practical training," Fred continues. "I'm a plasterer by trade." After high school, Fred worked at several jobs before he decided to go to college. Because he enjoyed working with people, he earned a diploma in special care counseling. He then earned a degree in social work.

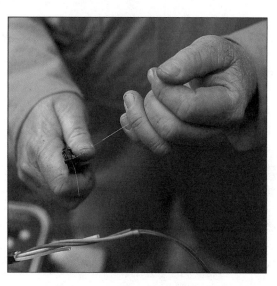

Some occupations are just beginning to develop, and have a good future. "One new occupation is in the area of fiber optics," Fred says. "Fiber optic cables are revolutionizing the communications industry in the same way that microchips revolutionized the computer industry." In the photograph, a technician is splicing the thin yellow strand of fiber optic cable.

How to become a tradesperson

"Many students interested in the trades take shop classes in high school. Others take general courses and gain experience through hobbies," Fred says. "Then, they work with someone who knows the trade well. People who want to become an apprentice are responsible for finding an employer willing to train them. A training consultant can really help people narrow the search for an employer.

"It's also a good idea to find a mentor," Fred suggests. "A mentor is someone you admire who is successful in at least one trade, and who is able to give you advice and inspiration. You don't have to be working toward the same trade as your mentor, but it's important that you share the same values."

Is this career for you?

Training consultants need to have a lot of energy. "You often deal with people who aren't sure what they want to do. You have to be enthusiastic as you encourage them to consider the possibilities open to them," Fred says.

"Many eligible employers don't think of taking on an apprentice," comments Fred. "It's true that taking on a trainee requires extra work and additional responsibility. But I encourage employers to see the positive side, too. They can train an apprentice to follow the specific routines of their own work place.

"It's extremely important to have good communication skills," he adds. "I often check that

David Hosick, a licensed mechanic, trained in welding and metal fabrication, and he also taught night classes. This combination of skills helps him when he designs and builds water systems in developing countries. He also trains local people to work with him.

I understand what has been said by repeating back exactly what I heard. Before repeating a client's words, I might ask, 'Are we rapping the same here?' or 'Are we on the same wavelength?' By using phrases that clients use with their friends, I make sure we understand each other.

"In this job, if you aren't organized, you're dead," Fred laughs. "The last thing I want to do is waste time looking for files. So I keep my files and information in order so I can focus on what's most important: helping people find jobs they enjoy."

Career planning

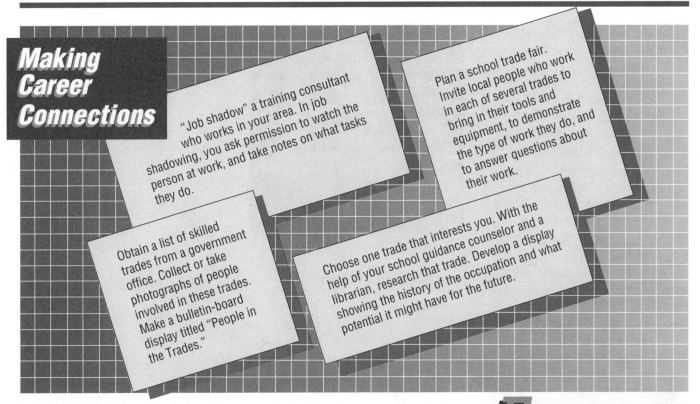

Making Career Connections

"Job shadow" a training consultant who works in your area. In job shadowing, you ask permission to watch the person at work, and take notes on what tasks they do.

Plan a school trade fair. Invite local people who work in each of several trades to bring in their tools and equipment, to demonstrate the type of work they do, and to answer questions about their work.

Obtain a list of skilled trades from a government office. Collect or take photographs of people involved in these trades. Make a bulletin-board display titled "People in the Trades."

Choose one trade that interests you. With the help of your school guidance counselor and a librarian, research that trade. Develop a display showing the history of the occupation and what potential it might have for the future.

Getting started

Interested in being a training consultant? Here's what you can do now.

1. Read trade magazines about trades that interest you.
2. Develop a positive attitude. Be ready to seize opportunities when they're offered. Fred recalls that he was once offered free training in the computer business. "I said 'no' without considering what I was being offered. Now I wonder what would have happened if I had said yes!"
3. Join the Junior Chamber of Commerce, 4-H, or some other community club. Develop a network of people who know you and your capabilities.
4. In high school, study English, mathematics, and science. Science courses will help you to understand new developments in the trades.

Related careers

Here are some related careers you may want to check out.

Human resources worker
Assists an employer in making hiring decisions. Advertises jobs and screens applicants. Interviews suitable job applicants, and helps to hire the best qualified ones. Also deals with employment matters, such as insurance.

Developmental services worker
Assists clients with learning disabilities to develop life skills. May deal with children or with adults. Works in schools, hospitals, or social service agencies.

Scheduler
Uses a data base to provide scheduling for various organizations, such as schools, job sites, and restaurants. This job requires good keyboarding skills, a knowledge of several computer programs, and an interest in trying to fit a schedule to people's needs.

Future watch

As long as people require job training, there will be a need for consultants to help them get that training. "Jobs like mine will change as different trades become more important in the changing job market," Fred explains, "and the job market is changing faster and faster! Skilled tradespeople of the future will need a combination of skills. For example, a welder might specialize in robotics, and have to learn about electronics."

Judy Wanless — Volunteer Coordinator

Many organizations, especially those that help people, require large numbers of volunteers. The volunteers are not paid for their work. Usually, however, the volunteer coordinator who organizes their activities is a paid employee. Judy Wanless is the volunteer coordinator for an organization that offers horseback riding lessons to people who have physical, mental, or emotional difficulties.

The riding facility that employs Judy is a non-profit organization. It raises just enough money to pay for its stables, horses, equipment, and a small staff. "We offer riding classes six days a week. We could never afford to pay for the amount of help we need," says Judy, "especially since each disabled rider may need up to five helpers." Instead, Judy has signed up 350 volunteers, who are trained to help the riders maintain their balance and control the horses they're riding.

Recruiting volunteers

Judy's job mostly involves contacting and scheduling enough volunteers for each riding session. "We need so many volunteers that I'm constantly looking for new ones," she says. A

Judy Wanless talks with a volunteer who works in the riding facility's barn. "I like to stay in touch with all the volunteers," Judy says. "We couldn't manage without them!"

local volunteer agency helps her find some. She also visits high schools to locate interested students.

Judy interviews new volunteers to find out about their skills and interests. Then she outlines the organization's expectations. "Each volunteer is asked to make a commitment of three to four hours per week, for 10 to 15 weeks," she notes. "We need 200 people a week!"

New volunteers attend an orientation session. "I greet them, show them around, and then I introduce them to a therapist or an experienced volunteer to learn our routines. After that, I schedule them into a riding class that needs sidewalkers. Other volunteers help organize and run our booths at local horse shows, they help develop public relations strategies, and they organize fundraising events."

"A rider who has poor balance has a 'sidewalker' on each side. These helpers prevent the rider from slipping sideways," Judy explains. "A physical therapist rides behind the saddle to help the rider maintain correct posture."

Public relations and paperwork

"I do a lot of public relations work, for example, producing brochures," Judy says. "I also talk to groups of young people, senior citizens, and business people, as well as people who come in to visit our facility because they're curious. I show them the facility, and explain what we're doing. Once they see the smile of delight when one of our clients learns how to ride, many of these visitors volunteer time or donate money."

"I help with fundraising by writing letters asking for donations," says Judy. "Every year, I plan a party at which we present special pins to people who have been with us for 5, 10, 15, or 20 years. Once a month, I ask the therapists to name the volunteer whom they think has worked especially hard. I put a picture of that volunteer on our 'What's Happening' bulletin board, along with a note of thanks."

Getting started

1. Volunteer to work with an organization that appeals to you. Talk to other volunteers to find out what motivated them to help others.
2. Develop interviewing skills by working for a school newspaper.
3. Join a public-speaking club.
4. Look for a part-time job in sales to gain experience working with the public.
5. In high school, take courses in English to improve your communication skills. Take any other courses in your school that will help you understand the feelings and behavior of other people.

Sean Finucan — Driving Instructor

"**D**river training starts in the classroom," explains Sean Finucan. "That's where we discuss a car's controls, traffic laws, and people's attitudes toward driving. Almost everyone who drives — whether 18 or 80 — could improve their driving attitudes," he notes. "I begin my classes by talking about the irritations that might affect a driver's attitude: a headache or an argument, a busy day, or being late. I always emphasize that it's better to be late than never arrive at all!"

To help students understand that they can adjust their attitudes, Sean demonstrates the difference between response and reaction. "Without warning, I toss a ball to a student, who automatically puts up a hand to try to grab the ball, but who usually misses. That's a *reaction*," he states. "Then I ask the same person to *prepare* to catch the ball. This time the student *responds*; the hands come up, and the ball is almost always

"You have to understand both cars and people to do a job like this," says Sean Finucan as he gets into the car he uses to teach people how to drive. Sean works for a company that provides young people with a safe introduction to driving.

caught. I point out to students that drivers must learn to be prepared for different driving situations, instead of simply reacting to them."

Behavioral choices

"Responding to driving situations means choosing from among several alternatives," Sean says. "I discuss with the students how different people make different behavioral choices. For example, imagine that someone is following too closely behind your vehicle. What would you do?"

During class sessions, Sean uses slides and videos so students can

Suppose you're driving along in a line of traffic, and you see a scene like this. What might happen next? Possibilities are on page 48.

learn from possible scenarios. "We'll discuss how different drivers might view the scene. That's when students begin to realize that they need to observe everything going on around them, and plan emergency responses, just in case."

On the road

"Once students have learned the basic information, it's time to go out and use it," Sean says. During each driving session, Sean evaluates what the student has learned. He writes comments on an evaluation sheet, and discusses them with the student after the session. "I try to be positive," he smiles. "I praise what was done well, and I explain what corrections need to be made, and why. Then we set a learning goal for the next lesson."

Getting started

1. Take a driver safety course.
2. Learn and follow traffic laws when bicycling.
3. If possible, learn how to drive a dirt bike or a motorized lawn mower. The steering is similar to that used in cars.
4. Join a sports team. As you get better, volunteer to coach younger players. This will help you acquire teaching skills.
5. Volunteer to tutor students who are having difficulties in your favorite subject. Strive to develop the patience needed by all teachers.
6. In high school, take courses in mathematics, physics, and auto shop to better understand how cars function. Also, take English courses to develop your communication skills.

Yvette James — Youth Worker

One of several youth workers in her community, Yvette James provides recreational, social, and cultural services to young people, mostly teenagers. She works for a community service agency similar to the one managed by Kevin Lee (see page 10).

"Working with young people is different from working with adults," explains Yvette. "For one thing, teens don't usually make appointments to talk with me. Instead, they drop by my office, or I notice someone on a park bench or in a donut shop who seems to need help. Because these meetings are often unplanned, I have to be flexible in how I schedule my time.

An advocate for youth

Sometimes, young people come to Yvette to discuss problems that involve other people or agencies. "A while ago, for example, 25 students got kicked out of the local high school," she recalls. "After talking with the students, I agreed to be their 'advocate' or representative. I contacted the school and discussed what the students had to do in order to return to classes. I also talked to their parents about the situation.

"During our discussions, I asked the students to agree simply to attend class," Yvette says. "And I offered to take them out to lunch if they brought me their report cards at the end of the term." Yvette's

request worked. "I knew that those who went to class would probably learn enough to pass," she comments. "Sure enough, the students who took me up on my offer got some As and Bs!

"I especially like helping young people see that they have the power to make changes," Yvette says. "Sometimes this is difficult, because teens often expect adults to do things for them. I like to challenge that idea.

"Last year, for example, we received some money from the government to educate 6- to 12-year-olds about drug abuse and drug prevention," Yvette explains. "We also needed jobs for local teenagers. So, I helped some teens develop a

Talking informally with young people about their needs and their goals is an important part of Yvette's job.

program that met both needs. The teens were hired to coach children's basketball as part of a program of drug-awareness. The program boosted the self-esteem of both the children and their teenaged coaches."

Family mediation

If a young client asks for help, Yvette might mediate a family dispute. "I sit down with the people who are having problems communicating," she says. "They might be a parent and a child, a brother and a sister, or a young couple. I listen to what each person has to say, and I help them develop solutions."

Yvette and Jason are joined by two of Jason's friends.

Getting started

1. Join clubs and committees at school, to gain experience working with different people.
2. Get involved in a conflict resolution program at your school.
3. Get a part-time job working with the public, for example in a store, in a library, or at a restaurant. You need patience and good listening skills when dealing with the public.
4. In high school, take courses in English and the social sciences, to improve your communication skills and your understanding of human behavior.
5. Sign up for volunteer or cooperative programs that involve hands-on work in your community.

Harry Bartz — Correctional Officer

What do correctional officers do? "Our main tasks are to maintain security and to see that the prisoners, or inmates, follow the routines," replies Harry Bartz. "What I like about this job," he adds, "is that I am always learning about how people — both my co-workers and the inmates — think and feel.

"The inmates are assigned to cells, two to a cell, and a number of cells make up a cell block," says Harry. "The inmates' cells are open for most of the day, and prisoners can talk to the others in their cell block, work, watch television, play games, write letters, or study. But they can't leave the cell block without a correctional officer.

"We lock up the cells in the evening, until it's time for inmates to get up in the morning," notes Harry.

Helping and supervising inmates

"We maintain a predictable daily routine," continues Harry. "For the most part all inmates are treated the same, from the clothes they wear to the food they eat. We introduce new inmates to this routine and help them to follow it.

"This part of my job enables me to supervise people, see how they

interact, and make sure that inmates are treated fairly. For example, some inmates try to harass others for extra food at meal times. When the food is brought up from the kitchen, we make sure that each inmate receives the correct type and quantity of food."

Prisoners can leave the cell block for certain activities. "For example, inmates have a scheduled exercise time," Harry comments, "and some have jobs in the kitchen or in the laundry. When they have a visitor, they're taken to a special visiting room. Prisoners can also leave the cell block for academic tutoring, training sessions, counseling or group therapy, or interviews with prison staff.

"The training and counseling sessions outside the cell block are extremely important to inmates," says Harry. "If they get work experience and job training, they can learn skills that may shorten their sentences — and keep them out of prison in the future."

Parole officers spend many hours helping former inmates land on their feet after they are released.

Harry Bartz works as a correctional officer in a prison.

Group dynamics

In his job, Harry has learned a lot about 'group dynamics,' or the ways in which people interact. He uses these insights to help inmates get along. "We can't oversee every inmate all the time," he explains. "But, we apply our knowledge of group dynamics to minimize conflicts among the prisoners. Noise levels tell us when something is going wrong," he continues. "In addition to regular checks, if it gets too noisy or too quiet, I need to see what's happening. Because I'm constantly alert to group dynamics, I often can sense when there's a problem brewing, and stave off trouble before it occurs."

Getting started

Interested in being a correctional officer? Here's what you can do now.

1. Join a cadets program or another group that teaches you self-discipline and self-control. This kind of experience will introduce you to the types of group dynamics that you will encounter in prison work.
2. Do activities that require you to follow step-by-step guidelines, and look for paid or volunteer work that involves attention to routines.
3. Exercise regularly and stay healthy and fit.
4. Learn First Aid, CPR, and other strategies for dealing with emergencies.
5. In high school, take courses in English, law, social studies, and physical education.

Classified Advertising

HELP WANTED

EXPANDING BUSINESS NEEDS PARTNERS
Full and part time. You are: ambitious, open-minded determined to SUCCEED. *No capital requirement.* Send resumé or note to: Box 42, 10020 Albert St. Missinabi, Province/State, Postal/Zip code

CANTONESE/ENGLISH BILINGUAL ACCOUNT EXECUTIVE
LEADING telecommunications company is currently expanding in the Oriental communities. Candidate should have at least 2 years sales and marketing experience in this country. Insurance and real estate experience are an asset. $40,000+. QUALIFIED applicants only. Please contact P[...] Dept. Manager, Mr. [...] daCosta at 555-0149

CREATIVE WRITER
Wanted for application [...] leading telecommunica[...] nology company. Exp[...] quired. Reply to VR [...] per. Box 400, The C[...] St[...] Keenan Blvd. City, P[...]nce[...] Postal/Zip Code

CITY DISPATCHER WANTED
Busy City dispatch requires innovative person to run local truck operation. Require good knowledge of ocean cargo. Apply in confidence to: GENERAL MANAGER P.O. Box 4329, New Amsterdam, Province/State, Postal/Zip Code

SALES REPRESENTATIVE

DUTIES:
Promote and sell b[...]ty window and de[...] products to the home b[...] market in the city.
QUALIFICATIONS:
• [...]imum three years sales experience in related field
• An understanding of the cus[...] tom home m[...] [...]

Pharmace[...]ical[...]

GRAPHIC ARTIS[...]
Our busy Advertisi[...] epartmer[...] and lay out flyers, p[...]ads and [...]
Your related coll[...] diploma is [...] rience that includes [...]liarity wit[...] QuarkXPress. You w[...] well und[...] priorities and can wo[...] deadline[...]
Please forward you[...] sumé to: ceuticals Trade 489 Su[...] view Ter[...] Zip Code Fax 555-4112 [...] qual opp[...]

ACTING INSTRUCTOR

Opeongo College requires a[...] Acting Instructor for the fall/winter academic year. This is a half-time position for a ten-month contract beginning mid August.
The Instructor will teach both Introductory and Intermediate Acting for 1st and 2nd year students. These courses are University Transfer recognized courses. Possible opportunities to direct College productions exists but is not a job requirement.
Bachelor's degree, acting and directing experience required. Master's degree in a related field preferred.
Deadline for application is June 25. Inquiries can be directed to the Personnel Department
**Opeongo College
450 9th Street
Southdown, Province/State**

[...]per[...] tram. Machin[...] Mechanical aptitude an asset. [...] command of English nec[...] Call ABC Wood, Ltd. 555-639[...] [...]intment
**Please call betw[...]
12 noon.**

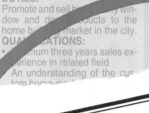

Summer Job Opportunity

Loon Lake Lodge requires a resident server for the summer. The successful applicant must be pleasant and helpful to guests, serve tables, and assist with cleaning the dining room during slow periods. Must be willing to work flexible shifts. Previous experience working with the public would be beneficial. High school or college students preferred. Mail or fax a resumé to:

Bernice Foley, Loon Lake Lodge
R.R. #5
Vacation City, Province/State
Postal/Zip Code; Fax: (222) 555-1689

Start Your Own Office Cleaning Business
Be your own boss, par[...] the evening [...]nks
[...]r complete information call 555-5190

FIRSTLINE HEALTH & RACQUET CLUB

Firstline Health & Racquet Clubs, expanding through Corrale and the surrounding area, offers an exciting and rewarding career in the health & fitness industry. We are currently searching for sales oriented individuals with strong interpersonal skills in the following positions.

1) Membership Consultant
2) Corporate Sales — must have corporate sales experience
3) Program Consultant
4) Cardio Tester

Qualifications:
- Minimum 2 years direct sales experience
- Background in aerobic & anaerobic training
- Knowledge of nutrition

Qualified applicants are invited to call Stan Florry for a confidential interview 555-1305 or fax your resumé to 555-1304

SCARBIN AND REDVILLE GENERAL HOSPITAL

Registered Nurses

In-patient Services
• Full and Part-time
An active acute care facility, the new In-patient Mental Health Department, will provide the experienced mental health care professional or professionals motivated to pursue career in mental health nursing with an ideal opportunity to broaden their group, interviewing, and counseling skills in a supportive and cooperative setting. The background of the ideal candidate will include recent experience in primary nursing care. General qualifications include a Certificate of Competence from the College of Nurses and [...] BCLS. File #43[...]

Recre[...] Therapist

In co[...]tion with the Occupational Therapist and pr[...] urses, you will dev[...] and implement recreati[...] [...] and activit[...] of all types to [...] individual patient ne[...] [...]ssessing p[...]nt leisure [...]rests, you will [...] [...]ions and pla[...]g com[...] [...]ions are availa[...] As the [...] year of experie[...] in an [...] recognized re[...]tion [...] nd Redville Ge[...] [...]ls dedicated to t[...] [...] invited to apply [...] Resources Office[...] [...] S. Scarbin, Prov[...]

[...]nager
[...]arpenter/Stage
[...]rpentry and [...]ce. In addi[...] [...]sound. The[...] [...]s and wi[...]
[...]vario[...]
[...]rmo[...]

[...] [...] [...]
[...]by July 9 to: Che[...] de M[...]ger, [...]n Center for Performin[...]04[...] [...]enue [...] rovince/State, Postal/Zip Cod[...]

[...]Weller[...]

JOURNEYMAN MACHINIST

General Machinist, preferably with milling experience required for precision machine shop manufacturing electromechanical sensors. Minimum 5-10 years related experience. Must be capable of reading detailed drawings and working to extremely close tolerances.
No telephone calls please. Forward resumés to:
**Mrs. P. Weller
Fred Weller Corporation
34 Leslie Road
Wellington, Province/State
Postal/Zip Code**

AWARDS FOR BUSINESS EXCELLENCE

Who got the job?

Finding a job

The first step to success in any career is getting a job. But how do you go about finding one?

- Talk with family, friends, and neighbors and let them know what jobs interest you.
- Respond to "Help Wanted" ads in newspapers.

- Post an advertisement of your skills on a community bulletin board.

- Register at government employment offices or private employment agencies.

- Contact potential employers by phone or in person.
- Send out inquiry letters to companies and follow up with phone calls.

A job application usually consists of a letter and a resumé (a summary of your qualifications and work experience, including volunteer work). After reading the letters and resumés submitted, an employer decides which applicants might be best qualified for the job, and asks them to come in for an interview.

Activity

Finding a summer job

Read the job advertisement on the opposite page, which appeared in a large city newspaper. What experience do you have that might help you get a summer job such as this?

Summer jobs that involve working and living at a tourist lodge are very popular. Because lodge owners frequently hire staff who live out of town, they often do their preliminary interviews by telephone.

Procedure

The letters and resumés submitted by two applicants — Pedro Kruz and Silvana Caparelli — are shown on pages 46 and 47. Read these letters and resumés. Make notes about whether each applicant might qualify for the job.

Both Silvana and Pedro were interviewed by telephone, then invited to a personal interview. Bernice Foley, the lodge owner, conducted the interviews and made notes about each applicant. Her notes are also shown on pages 46 and 47.

Consider each applicant's resumé and covering letter. Which candidate has the best qualifications and experience for this job? Then read the interviewer's notes about each candidate. If you were Bernice Foley, whom would you hire: Pedro or Silvana? What else, besides qualifications and experience, do you think Bernice would consider in making this hiring decision?

Challenge

How would you perform in a telephone interview? Role-play a telephone interview with a friend. Ask your friend to play the part of a lodge owner interviewing you for this job. Get your friend's feedback on how well you answered each question, and whether your telephone manner is direct and positive. If your friend points out problems in your response — for example, too many hesitations — continue to role-play telephone interviews until you improve. Then exchange roles with your friend.

Pedro Kruz's application and interview

34 Greenlaw Avenue
Barrville, Province/State
Postal/Zip Code

April 28, 19—

Bernice Foley
Loon Lake Lodge
R.R. #5
Vacation City, Province/State
Postal/Zip Code

Dear Ms. Foley,

WORLD-RENOWNED CHEF GETS START AT LOON LAKE LODGE

This could be a newspaper headline in the future if you hire me as your server!

For the past three years, I have worked in the school cafeteria. My job entails clearing tables, rinsing dishes, and running the dishwasher. I will be taking chef training next year, and would like to gain some experience in a professionally-managed dining room before I begin this training.

I am familiar with Loon Lake Lodge because my family and I vacationed there two summers ago. I would love to work at the Lodge for the summer. Please contact me at 555-3498 before 8:15 a.m. or after 8:30 p.m. to arrange an interview, at your convenience, should you consider my resumé appropriate.

Sincerely yours,

Pedro Kruz

Pedro Kruz
Enclosure

Interview: Pedro Kruz
- Arrived early. Wore a shirt and tie. Hair below shoulders.
- Why does he want the job? Wants to be a chef. Enjoys the country, would enjoy his time off.
- What would he do for a rude guest? Show to a table. Offer to take a beverage order.
- Good telephone manner
- Answers questions well
- Willing to work long hours

Resumé

Pedro Kruz
34 Greenlaw Avenue
Barrville, Province/State
Postal/Zip Code

Telephone: 555-3498

Education
I will complete high school this year. During the last semester, I excelled in a cooking class that included planning menus, shopping for and preparing foods, and serving tables.

Work Experience
Dishwasher: I have worked part time for three years in the school cafeteria. My duties include clearing tables, rinsing dishes, and running the dishwasher.

Hobbies and Interests
4-H: During the past four years, I have been Assistant Leader on eight projects, including Maple Syrup, Good Foods Fast, and Protecting Planet Earth.
Computer keyboarding: I have a large data bank of recipes I have collected, many of which I have prepared and served to family and friends.

References: Available on request.

Silvana Caparelli's application and interview

85 Avondale Avenue
Barrville, Province/State
Postal/Zip Code

May 1, 19—

Bernice Foley
Loon Lake Lodge
R.R. #5
Vacation City, Province/State
Postal/Zip Code

Dear Ms. Foley,

I wish to apply for the position of server which was advertised in the *Morning Gazette* on Thursday, April 27, 19—.

Currently, I work part-time for a local fast-food restaurant. I was hired for the job because the owners were impressed with my work during a high school Co-op program.

After my final year in high school, I am thinking about studying food and beverage management. I am interested in the job you have advertised because it will provide me with experience in this area. Please contact me before 8:15 a.m. or after 9:00 p.m. at 555-2997. I look forward to hearing from you, and would be very happy to meet with you in person, at any time that is suitable for you.

Sincerely,

Silvana Caparelli

Silvana Caparelli
(Resumé attached.)

Interview: Silvana Caparelli

- *On time. Wore a skirt and blouse. Long hair tied back neatly.*
- *Why does she want the job? To decide whether or not to study food management. Wants to earn money for college.*
- *How would she handle a rude guest? Show guest to a table. Bring water and menu. Describe the special of the day.*
- *Voice is quiet, difficult to hear.*
- *Pleasant manner, smiles frequently.*

Resumé

Silvana Caparelli
85 Avondale Avenue
Barrville, Province/State
Postal/Zip Code
Telephone: 555-2997

Job Experience

January 19— to present: Wobbley's Hamburger Hut, Highway 245, Barrville. Part-time counter server.

19— to present: Barrville Community Place, 78 Church Street, Barrville. Occasional weekend work rinsing dishes and running the dishwasher for community suppers.

19— to present: Various odd jobs, such as raking leaves, pet care, and snow shovelling for three neighboring families since I was 13.

Education

I am in my final year at Northwest High School in Barrville. My strong subjects include marketing, social studies, and Spanish.

Skills, Interests, and Awards

- Barrville Community Place: Five-year Volunteer Pin
- Second Place, Barrville Agricultural Society, Young People's Bake-Off
- Fluent in English and Italian

References: Available on request.

Index

Answers

Interested in interest? (see page 8)
At 7 percent, it would cost $3500 (0.07 x $50 000) per year to borrow $50 000. That is, if you borrowed $50 000 today, you would have to pay back $53 500 next year. You can learn about mortgage payments in math class.

Fred Brigham's list of occupations. He considers these when he asks clients the questions on page 35.
1. With people: hairstylist, home appliance service technician, funeral director, painter/decorator; alone: accountant, dry cleaner, editor
2. Indoors: auto body repairer, baker, cabinetmaker, cook, plasterer, watch repairer; outdoors: brick and stone mason, glazier, horticulturist
3. Sitting down: driver, mobile crane operator, printer, sewing machine operator; standing up: automatic machinist, camera operator, letter carrier, upholsterer
4. At heights: arborist, firefighter, tower crane operator
5. Underground: mine millwright, gasline pipefitter
6. With electricity: electrician, power lineworker, radio and television service technician

Sean Finucan's list (see page 41)
1. The car in front of you might slow down as the driver watches the children play.
2. A ball may roll into the path of your vehicle, and a child may come running after it.
3. Children may run across the road in front of you to leave or join the game.

Credits

(l = left; r = right; t = top; b = bottom; c = center; bl = bottom left; br = bottom right)

All photographs by Helen Mason, except 5, 6, 11(l), 11(c),

30(t) David Rising; 32(l) Regina Baur; 40(b) James E. McNeil.

All art by Warren Clark except 18(t) George King;